ARCHITECTURE TOURS L.A. GUIDEBOOK
PASADENA

Architecture Tours L.A. Guidebook
PASADENA

Laura Massino Smith

Schiffer
Publishing Ltd

4880 Lower Valley Road, Atglen, PA 19310 USA

DEDICATION

To my extraordinary husband, Drew, whose undying love, patience, encouragement, and support have guided me to discover my true passion.

Published by Schiffer Publishing Ltd.
4880 Lower Valley Road
Atglen, PA 19310
Phone: (610) 593-1777; Fax: (610) 593-2002
E-mail: Info@schifferbooks.com

For the largest selection of fine reference books on this and related subjects, please visit our web site at **www.schifferbooks.com**
We are always looking for people to write books on new and related subjects. If you have an idea for a book please contact us at the above address.

This book may be purchased from the publisher.
Include $3.95 for shipping.
Please try your bookstore first.
You may write for a free catalog.

In Europe, Schiffer books are distributed by
Bushwood Books
6 Marksbury Ave.
Kew Gardens
Surrey TW9 4JF England
Phone: 44 (0) 20 8392-8585; Fax: 44 (0) 20 8392-9876
E-mail: info@bushwoodbooks.co.uk
Website: www.bushwoodbooks.co.uk
Free postage in the U.K., Europe; air mail at cost.

Copyright © 2006 by Laura Massino Smith
Library of Congress Control Number: 2006923672

Designed by John P. Cheek
Cover design by Bruce Waters
Type set in Futura BdCn BT/Humanist 521 Lt BT

ISBN: 0-7643-2483-7
Printed in China

ARCHITECTURE TOURS L.A.

www.architecturetoursla.com
323.464.7868

Architecture Tours L.A. is a tour company that specializes in guided driving tours led by an architectural historian in a 1962 vintage Cadillac. Our tours focus on the historic and significant contemporary architecture in Los Angeles and highlight the cultural aspects of the history of the built environment in the city. This guidebook will allow you to drive yourself and go about discovering L.A. in your own car, at your own pace. In addition to PASADENA, other tours and books offered by Architecture Tours L.A. include:

HOLLYWOOD
SILVER LAKE
HANCOCK PARK/MIRACLE MILE
WEST HOLLYWOOD/BEVERLY HILLS
DOWNTOWN LOS ANGELES
FRANK GEHRY

Disclaimer

It is not advisable for anyone operating a motor vehicle to read this book. Please pull your car into a safe, designated parking area before attempting any fine print. Better yet, take this tour with a friend who can act as navigator and narrator. Naturally, the best way to see it all is riding shotgun with the author!

Neither the author nor the publisher assume responsibility for moving violations committed while intoxicated by this tour.

NOTE TO TOUR-GOERS

The sites included on this self-guided tour represent the architectural highlights of Pasadena. This tour is meant to be an overview, a starting point of sorts, of the City of PASADENA and is intended to give the participant a feeling for the city. By no means does the tour include EVERYTHING of interest. If it did you'd be driving for days. Instead, in a matter of hours you will have a pretty good understanding of PASADENA's historical and current architectural happenings. The photographs herein are for quick identification of what you will see in three dimensions on the tour. Please respect the privacy of all property owners. The criteria for inclusion are the historical, cultural, and architectural significances of each site and whether they can be seen relatively easily from the street. **So relax and have a great ride!**

INTRODUCTION

Just ten miles north of Los Angeles, Pasadena's earliest residents were the Hahamog-na Indians. Settling mainly in and around the Arroyo Seco, which means dry wash or gulch, it carried enough water for a small population of native people. While they also settled in other areas, many artifacts have been found in the Arroyo. Water from the mountains would run freely in the Arroyo, now enclosed in concrete. The Arroyo Seco is a natural feature now spanned by the Colorado Avenue Bridge. Part of it is now the location of the Rose Bowl stadium and other sporting activities, and part of it has been left in its natural state, used mostly for nature walks.

The Spanish explorers came here in the late 1700s and established the Mission San Gabriel to the east, on land which is now part of present-day Pasadena. The Spanish brought the Mexican population after the secularization of the Mission San Gabriel, and created the San Pasqual and San Rafael ranchos. These were farms that grew oranges and other citrus fruits that the Spanish had brought with them. They also cultivated vineyards, olives, and other crops.

In 1869 the Golden Spike was driven in Utah, where the Central Pacific and Union Pacific Railroads met – finally connecting California with the rest of the country and creating the transcontinental railway. Naturally, price wars broke out and kept ticket prices low. So low that almost anyone could afford to journey west, and many did. A surge in population coming from the Midwest and East ensued and Pasadena was incorporated by the "California Colony of Indiana" in 1886. They named it after the Chippewa Indian words for "Crown of the Valley" or "Valley between the Mountains." Many people came to Pasadena to escape the cold winters of their hometowns and stayed only during the winter months. People also came to Pasadena for health reasons. The dry, warm climate was thought to be very healthy and conducive to the healing of respiratory conditions.

Eventually, many of the people who came only for the winters decided to make permanent residences here. Many visitors also decided to retire here. These were mostly people who had already established businesses in the Midwest or East and had made their fortunes. William Wrigley, of the Chicago chewing gum business, came here, as did Adolphus Busch, the beer brewer of St. Louis, and many other wealthy industrialists. Other early residents of Pasadena included Andrew McNally, head of Rand McNally & Co., and astrophysicist George Ellery Hale, who developed the California Institute of Technology, with which great minds such as Albert Einstein and Linus Pauling were associated.

Since residents were not necessarily tending to business here, Pasadena evolved from an agricultural enclave to a resort town by the late 1880s. Elegant hotels were built for this vacationing population, including the Wentworth, The Hotel Green, and the Vista Del Arroyo, which are all still standing, now with different names. Cultural activities centering on music, art, and literature were prevalent then, and remain so today.

Capable architects were designing homes in the fashionable styles of the time and many excellent examples of Victorian architecture still exist here today. Various presidents visited Pasadena in these early years of the city. Presidents Hayes, Harrison, and Roosevelt all made trips here from the late 1880s to the early 1900s. At the turn of the century, the Arts & Crafts (Craftsman) style proliferated, and some of the finest examples are found here in the work of architects Greene & Greene, Alfred and Arthur Heineman, Louis Easton, and others. At this time, Orange Grove Boulevard was called "Millionaire's Row" because there were so many millionaires living there in grand mansions.

After World War I, the 1920s saw the advent of the new Art Deco style, as well as various revival styles, including Spanish Colonial and Mediterranean, American Colonial, French Provincial, and English Tudor. The bungalow court, a new concept in multi-unit dwellings was conceived and fully developed here. (One of the original courts with six units was actually moved to a new location in order to preserve it.) Many millionaires lost their for-

tunes in the 1930s during the Great Depression, and Pasadena's main commercial district on Colorado Boulevard took a downturn. In 1940, however, the Arroyo Seco Parkway (the 110 freeway) was built. This was the first in the system of freeways throughout southern California to be built. It connects Pasadena to Los Angeles and is a meandering highway that follows the natural contours of the Arroyo Seco.

Technological advancements are a part of Pasadena's history, too. The Jet Propulsion Laboratory (JPL) is located here, established by Cal Tech in the 1930s as part of NASA. The first satellite was created by JPL. It is the foremost organization dedicated to the exploration of the solar system and is responsible for creating the Mars Rover, which recently explored the surface of Mars.

After World War II, many of the outer lying suburbs developed, but Colorado Blvd.'s Old Pasadena commercial area fell deeper into disrepair. In 1969, the Cultural Heritage Ordinance was established by the city of Pasadena and restorations began. Currently nine landmark districts have been designated in the city and there are now over 3500 designated historic sites and districts. Preservation groups like Pasadena Heritage have worked tirelessly with the city to preserve the integrity of Pasadena's architectural treasures, to which this city is dedicated and committed to preserving.

4 Westmoreland Place

1) We start at the best-known landmark in Pasadena – The Gamble House. This retirement home was commissioned by David and Mary Gamble of the Procter and Gamble soap company. The house that soap built was constructed in 1908 by Pasadena-based architect brothers Charles Sumner Greene and Henry Mather Greene. It was designed in the Arts and Crafts, or Craftsman, style. The Arts & Crafts Movement of the early 1900s was a response to the ornate aesthetic and machine-made quality of Victorian architecture, which was dominant during the late 19th century. This movement was also a reaction to the insensitivity of the machine and the Industrial Age. The Arts and Crafts style originated in Europe and can be credited to William Morris in England, the father of the movement. Influences from America were Gustav Stickley, the furniture maker, and also *The Craftsman* magazine.

The Craftsman style of design is respectful of nature in its honesty of materials and sensitivity to landscaping, and elevates the human touch with its hand-made quality. Part of the Arts & Crafts movement was concerned with workers being taken advantage of in an increasingly industrial society. Many people longed to go back to the Medieval Period when there was a system of guilds and workers were unified. Another important aspect of the style was that the decorative arts, including furniture and lighting, be integrated into the overall design. Here at the Gamble House, the art glass of the front door depicts an oak tree, since they are common in the area. All of the furniture, lighting, rugs, stained glass, paneling, and landscaping were custom designed by the architects. Greene & Greene were masters of this style.

Some of the dominant characteristics of the Greenes' Craftsman style are low-pitched gabled roofs and widely overhanging eaves, exposed rafter tails, groupings of windows, wide porches, little (if any) applied ornamentation, the use of clinker bricks and boulders, terraces and sleeping porches, and dark woods and shingling on the exterior. On the inside, wood was used extensively. The dining room was usually the center of the house, often displaying elaborate woodwork with built-in wood carved breakfronts and cabinetry. Wood joinery was expressed honestly as it was meant to be exposed, and the extensive use of various woods including Oregon pine, redwood, oak, and fir added a warmth to the interiors. Colorful art glass was also used, sometimes creating an iridescent effect as seen in the front door of the Gamble House. Elements of the Japanese style, the English cottage, the Swiss chalet, and the Adirondack hunting lodge are all noted as influential to this style. All of these influences emphasize the relationship between the built and natural environments. These homes were meant to be comfortable, casual, practical, and to fit in to nature. To the right of the house is the original garage that now houses a bookstore.

1) The David B. Gamble House, 1908, Charles Sumner Greene & Henry Mather Greene, 4 Westmoreland Place

In 1966 the heirs of the Gamble family donated the house to the City of Pasadena and the University of Southern California School of Architecture. Students of architecture are specially chosen to live in the house for one year. A restoration of this house was completed in 2004.

The Gamble House has been designated a National Historic Landmark by the federal government, a Cultural Heritage Landmark by the City of Pasadena, and is also listed on the National Register of Historic Places.

The David B. Gamble House

The David B. Gamble House – Front Door

The Greene brothers were born in Cincinnati, Ohio in 1868 and 1870, but moved to St. Louis, Missouri in 1874. They also spent time living amongst nature in West Virginia at the family's farm. They came to California in 1893 to visit their parents, who had moved here a year earlier. Their mother had asthma and their father was not well either. They thought the mild climate of Pasadena would be beneficial to their health. Enduring a period of financial instability, coincidentally Mr. and Mrs. Greene moved in with relatives living here. Concerned about their parents, the sons moved to Pasadena from Boston, where they were practicing architects. Greene & Greene were educated at the Massachusetts Institute of Technology in Cambridge and worked for architecture firms in Boston, designing in the European Beaux-Arts style, which was fashionable at the time. They developed a unique California Craftsman style, however, after coming here. The last of their houses were built in the late 1920s after they moved out of the area.

There are more than fifty structures created by the Greenes in Pasadena. These buildings are protected by the City's Historic Treasure ordinance instituted in 1986 and are automatically looked upon as designated landmarks.

To the left of the Gamble House, behind the pine trees, is another home designed by the brothers:

2) This house was built before the Gamble House, as were most in this area. It was commissioned by Mr. and Mrs. Cole, who had come here from Minnesota for their retirement. Notice the distinctive use of a porte-cochere. This extension of the roof over the front entrance is stabilized by two large graduated columns made of boulders brought up from the Arroyo Seco. The immense chimney on the side of the house is also constructed of these boulders and gives the structure a strong sense of grounding, as if it were growing out of the earth. The newer box-like structure with the fish scale shingles houses the church, and the Cole House serves as the church offices.

2a) The Neighborhood Church, c. 1969, Smith and Williams

3) The Westmoreland Gates, 1917, Charles Sumner Greene & Henry Mather Greene

2) The John Addison Cole House (now Neighborhood Church), c. 1906, Charles Sumner Greene & Henry Mather Greene; c. 1969, Smith and Williams, 2 Westmoreland Place (301 North Orange Grove Blvd.)

 Now head north, back towards the Gamble House and look at the end of the driveway

3) The Westmoreland Gates, made of stones from the Arroyo, were also designed by Greene and Greene to further enclose the driveway for privacy.

 Exit and turn left onto Orange Grove Blvd. Pass Los Robles Avenue Pass Lake Avenue Turn left on Michigan Avenue

At the turn of the century, architects like Greene & Greene of Gamble House fame were just getting started with an architectural practice here and they perfected the California Craftsman home. Some of the other architects and designers working at this time were Timothy Walsh, brothers Alfred and Arthur Heineman, Louis Easton, and Grable & Austin. Most of these men built grand homes as you will see later, however, at the same time, contractors, builders, and developers were also building Craftsman style houses, but in a much more modest way. They were building houses for the middle classes, which were coming to Pasadena in larger and larger numbers at the turn of the 20th century.

As you approach the area now known as "Bungalow Heaven" you will see a neighborhood of very modest Craftsman houses built from approximately 1906-1914. Most of these homes were built either by builders, contractors, or their original owners. Many of the houses here are not credited to a particular architect, but to the developers and construction companies that built them. Most of the houses were built without the aid of an architect because books could be purchased with the plans and directions for do-it-yourselfers, or plans could be purchased from an architect or designer. As you will see, sometimes three houses in a row were built by the same developer. This could be thought of as the precursor to the suburban tract developments of the post World War II era. Many of the same building characteristics of the larger houses built for wealthy families in the Craftsman style are seen here. The emphasis of these designs was on the comfortable and casual family life. The homes were designed with the idea of integrating the house with the landscape.

The Bungalow Heaven neighborhood was declared a Landmark District in the mid-1990s and has one of the largest concentrations of intact Craftsman bungalows in the country. Currently one of nine Landmark Districts within the city of Pasadena, Bungalow Heaven also has the distinction of being the largest residential historic district in the United States with 1100 homes currently included. Landmark District status indicates that there is a conservation plan for the designated area regarding the exteriors. If owners want to alter the exterior of their house they must have the alterations approved by a design review board. Bungalow Heaven was annexed to the city in 1906. Many excellent examples are located within this district; just a few have been highlighted here. That many of the houses remain intact, or restored from when they were first built, is notable in the preservation of this neighborhood.

4) Here on the left side of the street is a house with a most unusual chimney where the front entrance to the house is. The chimney faces the street and is angled in a step-down brick pattern, making it the focal point of the facade. A cross-gabled roof, groupings of elongated rectangular windows, and very long shingling are typical of this style. Notice the slightly flared roof lines at either end suggesting a pagoda-like Asian influence.

4) Albert Mercer House, 1909, Guy S. Bliss – Builder, 875 North Michigan Avenue

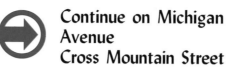

Continue on Michigan Avenue
Cross Mountain Street

5) Next, on the right side of the street is a house with two brick posts that also has a brick chimney in front. Here it does not become the focal point of the house, however, and the front door is not embedded into it. Typical Craftsman elements are the low pitched cross-gabled roof with one pitch facing the street and the other facing the side, and exposed rafter tails. Notable here is the presence of two Chinese Elm trees in the front yard, which feature prominently.

5) House, 1910, E.R. Zube – Builder, 938 North Michigan Avenue

6) Again on the right side of the street, directly next to the previous house is a bungalow with a stone porch, light brown shingles, and a cross-gabled roof that is asymmetrical as it faces the street. Exposed rafter tails and an exposed truss in the gable, as well as multiple rooflines add interest to the composition, and the stones used for the chimney create a unified design.

6) Margaret Langner House, 1910, E. R. Zube – Builder, 946 North Michigan Avenue

Continue on Michigan Avenue
Cross Bell Street
Cross Claremont Street

7) On the right side of the street there are three houses in a row. The two-story house painted green with maroon trim is called an "airplane bungalow." The characteristics of an airplane bungalow are the recessed second story, which is smaller than the first. It was named this because of the way the second story faces the street with the roof and exposed rafter tails resembling the lines of an airplane as though it had just landed on the rooftop. Groupings of windows and a large single pane picture window framed in simple, straightforward wood trim are also typical of the style.

8) Right next door is a most unique bungalow complete with a Dutch Colonial Revival style gambrel roof in front and repeated on the sides, decorative half-timbering, a three-sided bay window, clapboard siding, diamond pane windows, and an upper dormer window. The design of this house was influenced by the styles of the early Dutch and English colonies of the East Coast, a rarity in this neighborhood that provides exciting variety.

9) Next, on the right is a green painted house with cross-gabled roof. More of a pared-down design here with simple window frames, posts and materials, clapboard siding used below and shingling above, a leaded glass front door with a simple glass pattern and a wood ceiling above the porch. The landscaping complements the siting of the house.

7) H.H. Vincent House, 1910, J.K. Johnsen – Builder, 1276 North Michigan Avenue

8) House, 1912, M.R. Mitchell – Builder, 1282 North Michigan Avenue

9) House, 1915, M. R. Mitchell – Builder, 1292 North Michigan Avenue

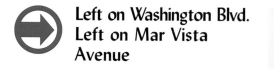

Left on Washington Blvd. Left on Mar Vista Avenue

10) Here on the left side of the street are three houses in a row that have unobstructed front yards and exemplify the "park-like" setting of the houses of Bungalow Heaven. The varied alternating shingle pattern almost resembles basket weave on this first house. Another interesting feature is the cross-gabled roof with a miniature gable in front.

Prominent architect Norman Foote Marsh (1871-1955) designed structures in Los Angeles and Pasadena. The Friendship Baptist Church here in Pasadena (which is listed on the National Register), South Pasadena High School, and Hollywood High School, among many other structures, most of which are not in the Craftsman style, were designed by this architect.

11) Right next door, this house also displays a cross-gabled roof, but with an additional flat roof over the porch. The squared cement posts may have been built up over the original wood or stone supports. The typical exposed rafter tails are here, but the alternating shingling adds visual depth to the surface.

11) House, 1912, Norman Foote Marsh, 1286 Mar Vista Ave.

10) House, 1912, Norman Foote Marsh, 1294 Mar Vista Ave.

12) And next to that is a house distinguished by brick posts flanking a white fence. The window groupings are somewhat unusual because there are five windows together instead of two or three, allowing more light into the house and adding a touch of subtle variety.

12) House, 1912, Norman Foote Marsh, 1278 Mar Vista Ave.

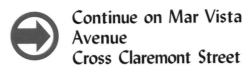

Continue on Mar Vista Avenue
Cross Claremont Street

13) Here on the right side of the street is a house with a brown fence in front and mature landscaping, creating a very private front porch. This is where the Nobel Prize winner Linus Pauling lived at one time when he was affiliated with research at Cal Tech.

13) House, c. 1910, (architect/builder unknown), 1141 Mar Vista Ave.

14) House, 1914, William Powell – Architect/Builder, 1002 North Catalina Ave.

Right on Bell Street
Left on Catalina Avenue

14) Right here at the corner on the left side of the street is a two-story house with large eucalyptus trees in front. Another airplane bungalow, the asymmetrical rooflines on the first story with a cross-gabled roof over the front porch are oriented to the left. The front door is decorative with vertical inset glass panes and a wood band support. Vents are decorative, too. The second story glassed-in room may have been an open sleeping porch at one time. Mature trees create a feeling of integration of nature with a made-man structure.

Quick left on Mountain Street
Quick right on Catalina Avenue

15) Here on the right is a most unique two-story house with Arroyo stone arches on the corners of the house set on the diagonal. This house may have started in the Victorian style and has been altered over the years. The unusual way the second story is larger than the first adds a precarious element to the house and variety to the neighborhood.

15) A.A. Thralls House, c. 1900, relocated 1906, (architect/builder unknown), 771 North Catalina Ave.

Right on Orange Grove Blvd.
Pass Lake Avenue

16) No longer in the district of Bungalow Heaven, here on the left side of the street at the corner of El Molino Avenue is a large Craftsman style house. It exuberantly shows the Japanese influence in the flared rooflines and features boulders from the Arroyo as posts to support the roof above the wraparound porch. Typical Craftsman features, such as exposed rafter tails and plain wood trim around the windows, are exaggerated here. The window trim is tapered towards the ground echoing the shape of the house as it touches the earth, creating the feeling of growing out of the ground. The use of boulders mixed with clinker bricks is also striking, and the numerous windows allow for easy access to nature. This house is listed on the National Register of Historic Places.

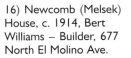

16) Newcomb (Melsek) House, c. 1914, Bert Williams – Builder, 677 North El Molino Ave.

Newcomb (Melsek) House

Continue on Orange Grove Boulevard

17) Next on your left, at the corner of Oakland Avenue, is the Orange Grove Friends' Meeting House, the Quaker Meeting Religious Society of Friends. The somber white and grey building features a very steep roof, a prominent chimney, exposed rafter tails, and Gothic-inspired pointed arch vertical vents. Clapboard siding is used here, too. It was designed for the Quakers and the original part of the building is the section on the right. The addition on the left was built after World War II. First established in Pasadena in 1882, this is the only Quaker Meeting House in the city and they have a congregation of approximately one hundred members.

17) Orange Grove Friends' Meeting House, the Quaker Meeting Religious Society of Friends, c. 1909, C. E. Manning – Builder, 520 East Orange Grove Blvd.

Continue on Orange Grove Blvd.
Pass Fair Oaks Avenue
Cross the Freeway
Right on Pasadena Avenue
Pass Hickory Lane

18) Here on your left is an example of preservation at its best. This charming bungalow court was actually moved here from Madison Street in central Pasadena. The bungalow court concept was invented in Pasadena. It was an alternative to suburban developments and arranged the housing so the units faced each other and shared a central courtyard. A family could live in a freestanding home, or sometimes attached, with their own front door. A sense of privacy and individuality was created, as well as a sense of community with neighbors. There are six units in all here, four of which are freestanding and two at the back that face the street and share one wall. Separate garages are located in back of the houses. Stones from the Arroyo are used for the chimneys and low garden walls. This bungalow court was designed in a combination of English Tudor Revival and Craftsman styles, combining the half-timber method of the English Tudor style with Craftsman shingles. White columns in front add a touch of the Colonial or Neoclassical style, too. A beautiful green lawn in the center and on the sides provides a natural setting for these homes, creating a sense of tranquility. There are more than 100 of these courts in Pasadena. This complex is listed as a Cultural Heritage Landmark by the City of Pasadena. This complex is also listed on the National Register of Historic Places.

18) Gartz Court (originally Gloria Court), 1910, Matthew Slavin, 745 North Pasadena Ave.

Gartz Court

Turn around to go back out on Pasadena Avenue
Right on Orange Grove Blvd.
Right on Rosemont Avenue
Right on Prospect Sq.

This lovely street lined with mature camphor trees is part of the neighborhood called Prospect Park. This area is a historic district known as "Prospect" and is listed on the National Register of Historic Places.

Left on Prospect Blvd.
Left on Prospect Crescent

19) Your next site is that of American master architect Frank Lloyd Wright. The Millard House, also known as "La Miniatura" because of its diminutive scale, was built for a dealer of rare books. Alice Millard was from Chicago and had a storefront bookstore in Pasadena, but kept some of her books here at home as well. The house was constructed using the textile block method devised by Frank Lloyd Wright, and is one of four houses in the Los Angeles area using this method. This type of construction required molds for the textured concrete blocks, which were then strung together with steel reinforcing rods. The others are in Hollywood, Los Feliz, and West Hollywood, and were also built in the early 1920s. Son of Frank Lloyd Wright, Lloyd Wright added a small studio to the back of this home in 1926. This house is listed on the National Register of Historic Places.

19) Millard House (a.k.a. "La Miniatura"), 1923, Frank Lloyd Wright, 645 Prospect Crescent

Continue around the bend
Right on Prospect Blvd.

20) The Bentz House here on your right, at the corner of Prospect Blvd. and Prospect Crescent, is another by Greene & Greene. The house was surfaced in deep chocolate brown, or "dirt" brown shingles to blend in with its surroundings. This house is listed on the National Register of Historic Places.

20) Bentz House, 1906, Charles Sumner Greene & Henry Mather Greene, 657 Prospect Blvd.

21) At the end of the street are the gates called the Prospect Park Portals. Also designed in the Craftsman style, the gates were constructed with clinker brick and boulders from the Arroyo, and make the neighborhood that much more exclusive. Clinker bricks were made irregular in shape by exposing them to hotter temperatures by putting them very close to the heat source when they were manufactured. This gave them a handcrafted appearance.

The houses here on your left were all designed by Greene & Greene. This area is a historic district known as "Park Place/Arroyo Terrace," and is listed on the National Register of Historic Places.

22) The first house on the corner to your left was built for Mary Ranney. Mary Ranney's name is on the drawings for this house because she worked as a draftsperson for Greene & Greene. This was her own house and after it was finished she continued to work for the architects. The house itself has been placed diagonally on the lot to relate to its corner site.

21) Prospect Park Portals, c. 1908, Prospect Blvd. at North Orange Grove Blvd.

**Right on Orange Grove Blvd.
Right on Arroyo Terrace**

22) Ranney House, 1907, Charles Sumner Greene & Henry Mather Greene, 440 Arroyo Terrace

23) Next door, the Willet House was originally built in 1905 and was completely remodeled in 1927 in the popular Spanish Colonial Revival style of that time. It was built for a Judge Willet with just one story. Little remains of the original house.

24) Next door again is the Hawks House, which belonged to the father of movie producer Howard Hawks. Hawks was from Indiana and produced films including "The Big Sleep" and "Gentlemen Prefer Blondes." He had this house built for his father. Notice how the driveway becomes a decorative element with its extensive brick and stone construction. The attention to detail in the construction of the stone walls and chimneys was something that the architects took very seriously and often meticulously chose particular stones for particular places.

23) Willet House, 1905, Charles Sumner Greene & Henry Mather Greene, 424 Arroyo Terrace

24) Frank W. Hawks House, c. 1906, Charles Sumner Greene & Henry Mather Greene, 408 Arroyo Terrace

25) The Van Rossem-Neil House was started in 1903 and later remodeled. It was originally built as a rental property for Mrs. Van Rossem, one of three houses in the area designed by Greene & Greene for her, and was remodeled and altered at the request of Mr. James W. Neil in 1906. With the remodeling, shingles were put over original clapboard siding. Notice the wave pattern of the brick and stone wall in front.

Look to your right down the path on the left side of the church to see the enormous boulders of the chimney of the Cole House seen earlier.

25a) Cole House – Stone chimney

26) Directly adjacent is the White Sisters' House. Martha, Violet, and Jane were the sisters-in-law of Charles Greene, and the house was designed for them. Notice how the shape of the house reflects the curve of the street.

25) Josephine Van Rossem-Neil House, 1903, Charles Sumner Greene & Henry Mather Greene, 400 Arroyo Terrace

26) White Sisters' House, 1903, Charles Sumner Greene & Henry Mather Greene, 370 Arroyo Terrace

27) Next is Charles Sumner Greene's own house. It is unusual in its form and reflects additions and expansions made at different times. Projecting bays and a hexagonal room on one end add to its unique quality. Charles Greene's personal studio was on the second floor and he used this house to test new design ideas. The stunning decorative stone and brickwork on the exterior exemplify the attention to detail for which the Greenes were known. The garage doors have been remade and are a replica of the originals. This was the first use of stones from the Arroyo and clinker brick, now seen in so many of the Greene & Greene houses.

27) Charles Sumner Greene House "Oakholm" – Garage doors and stone wall

Charles Sumner Greene House "Oakholm," c. 1902, Charles Sumner Greene & Henry Mather Greene, 368 Arroyo Terrace

28) On your right, down below the fence and in the distance is the Rose Bowl stadium, designed in 1922 by Myron Hunt in an elliptical shape. It has undergone a number of alterations throughout the years, but is still the site of the famous New Year's Day football game which takes place after the Tournament of Roses parade. The first "Festival of Roses" Parade took place in 1890 and was called "Battle of the Flowers." Horse-drawn carts adorned with flowers were used in the parade. Afterwards games were played and races were run, including chariot races. This was done every year as a way to show the world the good weather here on January 1st as it was publicized in Eastern and Midwestern newspapers. In 1902 the first football game was held and has been the tradition ever since. The stadium was originally horseshoe shaped and has been expanded a number of times; it now holds more than 100,000 people. Beneath you is also the Brookside Park, with the Aquatic Center and playing fields. It was named Brookside after Mrs. Everett Wellington Brooks, the wife of a manufacturer from Chicago, who financed the "Brookside Plunge" pool, which is now called the Aquatic Center. The Rose Bowl is listed on the National Register of Historic Places and has been designated by the federal government as a National Historic Landmark.

28) Rose Bowl, 1922, Myron Hunt, 991 Rosemont Blvd. (1001 Rose Bowl Drive)

Rose Bowl – As seen through fence

29) On the left corner of Arroyo Terrace and Grand Avenue is the house that was originally for Katherine Duncan and was moved to this location at her request. It was a very modest one-story cottage built by an unknown architect. She had it enlarged in 1903, but shortly thereafter Theodore Irwin purchased the house and with the help of Greene & Greene it underwent a major remodeling and expansion in 1906 for his growing family. Only one room of the original house remains. This house is more varied than some of the others and has a remarkable quality of integration of landscape and siting. The two-story house is built around a central open courtyard complete with fishpond. More of a Japanese influence is also seen here. This house was recently restored in 1983. This house is listed on the National Register of Historic Places.

Continue on Arroyo Terrace

30) The more recent condominiums designed here by a local firm, whose original principals were Conrad Buff III and Donald Hensman (a.k.a. Buff, Smith and Hensman, later). They designed several multi-unit dwellings and single family homes in the area. Although not mimicking the surrounding architecture, the composition blends into the neighborhood by existing subtly and unobtrusively. This style also reflects that of the time period and the pure simplicity of the International Style, though not as severe as its predecessors in Europe.

31) On your right as the road curves is a magnificent English Tudor Revival style house complete with a gardener's cottage on the grounds. It was originally owned by the Holmes Family until circa 1927 and then by the Newcombs into the 1940s. Various architects' names were found on the original documents, including the Castle Company for the construction of a garage in 1922, G. Lawrence Stimson for the removal of doors and the construction of a mantel in 1938 and 1939, and Myron Hunt and H.C. Chambers for enlargements and alterations in 1940. It is possible that the plans for this house were purchased from an architect, but it is not conclusive.

29) Duncan-Irwin House, 1900, (architect unknown); 1906 Expansion and remodel, Charles Sumner Greene & Henry Mather Greene, 240 North Grand Ave.

30) Arroyo Terrace Condominiums, 1979, Buff and Hensman, 200-236 Arroyo Terrace

31) Holmes Family/James G. Newcomb Estate, 1910, 1922, (architect unknown), 141 North Grand Ave.

Left on Grand Avenue

32) On your right is the Myron Hunt House, which was designed by the architect for himself. The house displays the architect's own version of the Craftsman style, with shingles on the second story and stucco on the first. Classical columns in front and leaded glass diamond pane windows reflect more of an English influence. The front door is on the side of the house that faces away from the street.

Myron Hunt was educated at the Massachusetts Institute of Technology, then worked in Chicago, where he knew Frank Lloyd Wright. He traveled in Europe before coming to California in 1903. Myron Hunt came here from Evanston, Illinois because his wife was suffering from tuberculosis. The air in Pasadena was thought to be healthful for those suffering from respiratory conditions. Hunt was one of the first members of the Pasadena Chapter of the American Institute of Architects. He also had working associations with Elmer Grey and H.C. Chambers. Myron Hunt died in 1952 at the age of 84 in this house. In Pasadena he designed the Rose Bowl, some buildings of the Huntington Estate, the Wentworth (now Ritz-Carlton Huntington) Hotel, the Elks Club, the Pasadena Library, some buildings

of the Cal Tech campus, the Casita Del Arroyo, as well as many others. He was a very prolific architect in Pasadena and also designed the Ambassador Hotel in Los Angeles where Robert F. Kennedy was assassinated. This house is listed as a Cultural Heritage Landmark by the City of Pasadena.

32) Myron Hunt House, 1904, Myron Hunt, 200 North Grand Ave.

33) George Edward Hutchins House, c. 1895, relocated 1904, (architect unknown), 206 North Grand Ave.

33) Next door is the Hutchins House on your right, which was moved from another location in this neighborhood in 1904 by the second owner. This typical Queen Anne Victorian style house is an example of what the Craftsman philosophy was responding to. The machine-made surface decoration, fish scale shingles and turned wood spindles of the railing are all standards of the Late Victorian style. Oriented in a vertical fashion and very tall, it is the antithesis of Craftsman architecture and provides an excellent setting to compare the various styles. This house has been beautifully restored and maintained. This house is listed as a Cultural Heritage Landmark by the City of Pasadena.

34) Next on your right is the second house built for Mrs. Van Rossem by the Greenes. She worked in real estate and it was built for a client coming from the East. Notice the large front facing gable alluding to the Swiss Chalet style.

35) Across the street, on the left behind the hedge wall, is the James Culbertson House first started in 1902 by the Greenes. At that time it was an English Tudor Revival style two-story house with steeply pitched roofs and walls of stucco and shingles. In 1955, this house was extensively re-modeled and the only remains are the stones and clinker bricks. The Culbertsons were from Chicago and another of the family's homes will be seen later.

35) James Culbertson House, 1902, Charles Sumner Greene & Henry Mather Greene, 235 North Grand Ave.

34) Josephine Van Rossem House II, 1904, Charles Sumner Greene & Henry Mather Greene, 210 North Grand Ave.

36) Again, on your right is another house designed by Myron Hunt with Elmer Grey. The recently restored Speer House was designed in the Dutch Colonial Revival style. Unusual to see here, this style flourished on the East Coast where the original Dutch colonies were. The distinctive gambrel roof adds more livable space to the second story, as do the dormer windows.

And again on your right is the Duncan-Irwin House.

The Duncan-Irwin House

36) John E. Speer House, 1904, Myron Hunt and Elmer Grey, 230 North Grand Ave.

**Right on Arroyo Terrace
Right on Orange Grove
Blvd.**

37) The Pasadena Museum of History, on your left at the corner of Walnut Street and Orange Grove Blvd., is now housed in what was originally the Fenyes House. Designed for Dr. Adalbert and Eva Fenyes and their family in the Beaux-Arts, or Neo-classical style, it is one of the few remaining grand mansions on Orange Grove Blvd., which was known as "Millionaire's Row," during the early 1900s. The house served as the headquarters of the Finnish Consulate from 1946-1970 because the daughter of the original Fenyes family was married to the gentleman representing the Finnish Consul for the Southwest. In the back there is a Finnish country house complete with a sauna and folk art. A collection of California Plein Air paintings are also housed here, as well as an excellent library with research materials concerning the history of Pasadena. This building is listed as a Cultural Heritage Landmark by the City of Pasadena. It is also listed on the National Register of Historic Places.

37) Fenyes House, (now Pasadena Museum of History), 1905, Robert D. Farquhar; 1911 addition, Sylvanus Marston, 170 North Orange Grove Blvd. (470 West Walnut Street)

38) The Late Victorian style house on the right hand corner of Holly Street was designed by Frederick Roehrig, who also designed the Hotel Green, which you will soon see. It was built at the turn of the century and is in pristine condition. This house was originally located on Los Robles Avenue and was moved to its current site in 1987 followed by an extensive restoration.

39) On your left on the corner is the War Memorial Flagstaff designed by Bertram Goodhue, who also designed the Central Library in Downtown Los Angeles, as well as other structures. It was created to honor veterans of World War I. This structure is listed as a Cultural Heritage Landmark by the City of Pasadena.

38) Mary Stowell House, 1895, Frederick L. Roehrig, 107 North Orange Grove Blvd.

39) War Memorial Flagstaff, 1927, Bertram G. Goodhue, corner of Orange Grove Blvd. and Colorado Blvd.

Left on Colorado Blvd.

40) The Norton Simon Museum (originally the Pasadena Art Museum), here on your left, was designed as a sculptural form. The structure is clad in deep umber handmade tiles designed by artist Edith Heath. The color of the tiles changes as the intensity of the sun reflects upon them throughout the day. The dark color is meant to relate to the dark color of the Craftsman style houses in the neighborhood. The rounded corners and the meandering shape were conceived as an abstract Modern sculpture and meant to be part of the art experience of the museum. The interiors were renovated in the late 1990s by architect Frank Gehry's firm.

Norton Simon was a successful businessman and his holdings included Max Factor Cosmetics, Canada Dry Corporation, McCall's Publishing, and Avis Car Rental, to name a few. He was married to actress Jennifer Jones in 1971 and they amassed an excellent collection of art. Housed here is a varied collection including Impressionist paintings, Indian and Southeast Asian art, prints and etchings, and sculpture. Norton Simon died in 1993.

40) Norton Simon Museum, 1969, Ladd and Kelsey, 411 West Colorado Blvd.

41) Across the street, the large white structure is the Pasadena Elks Lodge, which was designed to look very traditional, like Mount Vernon or a Southern plantation house. A row of striking neoclassical white columns in front precedes two rows of windows with shutters, replicating the Colonial Revival style.

41) Pasadena Elks Lodge, c. 1911, Myron Hunt and H.C. Chambers, 400 West Colorado Blvd.

Continue on Colorado Blvd.

42) You are now driving through Old Pasadena, or Old Town, which was originally lined with brick and wood Victorian-era buildings. Colorado Boulevard was the first commercial district in Pasadena and most of the structures were built from 1876-1900. In 1929 Colorado Boulevard (originally called Colorado Street) was widened and many of the old buildings were replaced with brick or concrete buildings in the Spanish Colonial Revival style or the Art Deco style popular at that time. With the widening of the street, fourteen feet were literally cut off from the front of the original buildings and the new structures were built on top of that.

The architectural styles most prominent during the 1920s and 1930s were Art Deco and Spanish Colonial Revival and many excellent examples survive here. The Art Deco style gets its name from an exhibition in the 1920s in Paris called, loosely translated, The Exposition of Industrial and Decorative Arts. The visual characteristics of this style are angular and geometric forms and highly decorated surfaces. The chevron, or flattened V-shape, is frequently seen, as are the sunburst pattern and stylized floral forms. The Spanish Colonial Revival style refers back to the Spanish colonization of California. Surfaces are usually copiously decorated with scroll forms, shield shapes, victorious wreaths and idealized soldiers, referring to the military power of Spain. Architects Bennett & Haskell designed many of the facades in the 1920s. As early as the 1930s, after the stock market crash of 1929, however, the area began to fall into decline. After another commercial district was built on Lake Avenue, which took much of the business away from here, Colorado Boulevard declined even further. By the 1970s, there were plans to demolish some of the buildings here, but preservationists fought to save the older buildings. In the mid-1970s, Pasadena Heritage, a local preservation organization, stopped the deterioration and demolition and made it financially feasible to rehabilitate the buildings by offering tax credits. The area has come back to life and is currently very lively. Today the area has been designated as an Urban Conservation Zone by the city of Pasadena. This area is also a historic district known as "Old Pasadena" and is listed on the National Register of Historic Places.

42) Old Pasadena, Colorado Blvd. – Spanish Colonial Revival Style

42a) Old Pasadena, Colorado Blvd. – Art Deco Style

42b) Old Pasadena, Colorado Blvd. – Art Deco Style

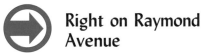 **Right on Raymond Avenue**

43) Coming up on your right is the very grand Hotel Green, now a privately owned residence called Castle Green. Commissioned by Colonel George G. Green, it was designed by architect Frederick Roehrig. The fact that the Santa Fe train station was nearby added to the convenience of the hotel's location for many visitors. Designed in an eclectic style combining elements of the Spanish Mission Revival style with Moorish decoration and details, it is one of the most unique buildings in Pasadena. The building across the street was once part of the hotel, as the facility was enlarged three times to accommodate the burgeoning population. The bridge connected the two buildings. The towers are dramatic, as are the barrel shaped protrusions of the structure. Intricate applied decoration adorns the surface of the building and some of the window glass is curved. Hotel Green was the setting for many events, and President Benjamin Harrison visited the hotel in 1891.

Architect Frederick L. Roehrig was born in New York and educated at Cornell University. He came to Pasadena in 1883 and was a member of the California State Board of Architecture and the American Institute of Architects. This building has been used in films including *The Sting* and *Bugsy*. Now lived in by permanent residents who own their homes, twice a year near Christmas time and Mother's Day, Castle Green opens up and the public is invited to tour the former hotel. This building has been designated a Historic Monument by the city of Pasadena. This building is also listed on the National Register of Historic Places.

43) Hotel Green (now Castle Green),
1887, 1898, 1903, Frederick L. Roehrig,
50 East Green Street (99 South
Raymond Ave.)

Hotel Green (now
Castle Green)

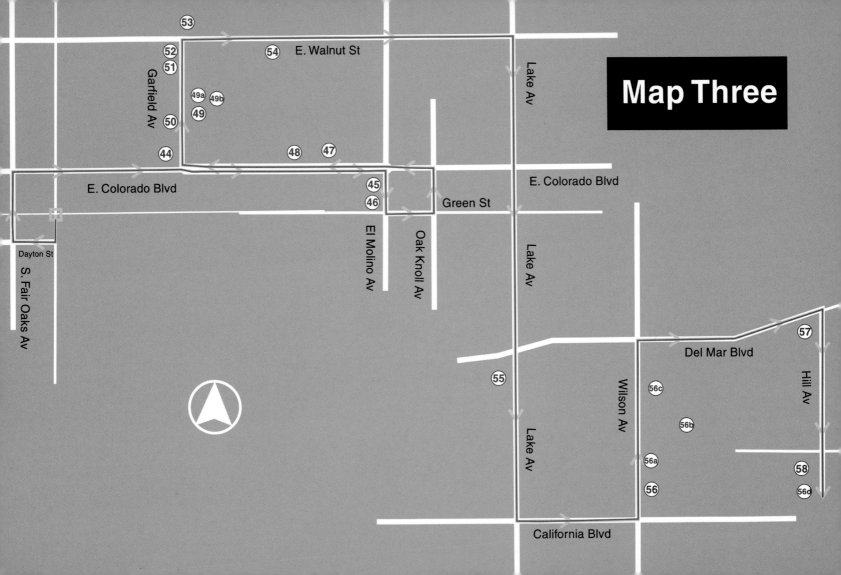

Map Three

Right on Dayton Street Right on Fair Oaks Avenue Right on Colorado Blvd.

44) On your left, at the corner of Garfield Avenue is the United States Post Office. Designed in the Mediterranean Italian Renaissance Revival style, characterized in part by the repeated arches, it is beautiful outside, but spectacular on the inside with polychrome terra cotta tiles and pristine grillwork. It was thought to be exorbitant for the government to build something so lavish and showed a great respect for the city of Pasadena by the government to do so. In the late 1990s this building was restored and seismically upgraded. This building is listed on the National Register of Historic Places.

44) United States Post Office, 1914, Oscar Wenderoth; 1938 addition, Sylvanus Marston, 281 East Colorado Blvd.

Continue on Colorado Blvd. Right on El Molino Avenue

45) Next, on your right is the Pasadena Playhouse. It was designed and built in the mid-1920s in the California Mission Revival style by an architect who sometimes partnered with Myron Hunt. Elmer Grey also designed the Beverly Hills Hotel in 1912 and other structures in the region. This was the first theater in America to stage Shakespeare's thirty-seven plays and was proclaimed the State Theater of California. It was opened in 1925. The design concept for the two-story Pasadena Playhouse uses the traditional style of the Spanish missions with an open courtyard patio in front and the main building directly behind it. This building is listed as a California Registered Historical Landmark and is also listed on the National Register of Historic Places. This area is also a historic district known as "Pasadena Playhouse" and is listed on the National Register of Historic Places.

45) Pasadena Playhouse, 1925, Elmer Grey, 39 South El Molino Ave.

Continue on El Molino Avenue

46) Next, on your right at the northwest corner of El Molino Avenue and Green Street is the Jacob Maarse florist, originally a Cadillac car dealership. The Cadillac insignia can be seen in the center of the decorative tile work above the entrance.

46) Cadillac Car Dealership (now Jacob Maarse Florist), 1925, Marston, Van Pelt and Maybury, 655 Green Street

47) Pasadena Presbyterian Church, 1976, John Gougeon, 585 East Colorado Blvd.

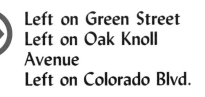 **Left on Green Street Left on Oak Knoll Avenue Left on Colorado Blvd.**

47) Coming up on your right at the corner of Madison Avenue, is the strikingly modern Pasadena Presbyterian Church. The original church that was located here was torn down after it suffered extensive earthquake damage in the early 1970s. The church exterior is an enormous abstract sculptural form clad in plaster with embedded rock in soaring shapes creating a very strong dramatic feeling. Inside, the red oak parquet floors and cedar ceiling have a warmth that complements the 72-foot high stained glass window above the altar. The shape of the window is that of a slender inverted Gothic arch, which makes a very dramatic statement ascending to the heavens as it alludes to traditional church architecture.

 Continue on Colorado Blvd.

48) On the right side of the street, just past Oakland Avenue, is the storefront of Linden Optometry, originally the Warner Building, which first housed upscale shops. The glazed ceramic molded green decoration is sumptuous in its richness of form and color. This kind of lavish decoration characterizes the height of the Art Deco period of the 1920s.

48) Warner Building, (now Linden Optometry), 1927, Marston and Maybury, 477 East Colorado Blvd.

Continue on Colorado Blvd.
Right on Garfield Avenue

49) The Civic Center is ahead of you here and was built in and around 1927 with City Hall as the focal point. It was designed in the Classical European, Italian Renaissance, or Beaux Arts style. These architects also designed the City Hall in San Francisco and were chosen from a design competition for the Civic Center complex. The dome is strikingly grand in scale and impressively sited. The grounds towards the back of the building have been

left "unfinished" in their natural state. A path of sand surrounding a fountain and sitting areas, as well as an arcade, are reminiscent of the early California missions. This building is listed as a Cultural Heritage Landmark by the City of Pasadena. This building is also listed on the National Register of Historic Places. This area is a historic district known as "Pasadena Civic Center" and is listed on the National Register of Historic Places.

49) Pasadena City Hall, c. 1927, John Bakewell and Arthur Brown, 100 North Garfield Ave.

49a) Pasadena City Hall

49b) Pasadena City Hall

50) The bronze sculpture across the street depicts Pasadena residents and brothers Jackie and Mack Robinson. They were both athletes. Mack won a silver medal in the 1935 Olympics in the 20-meter dash and Jackie Robinson was the first African-American to play on a major league baseball team and was with the Brooklyn Dodgers in 1947. They grew up here and both attended local schools.

50) Pasadena Robinson Memorial Sculpture, 1997, corner of Garfield Ave. and Holly Street, Ralph Helmick, Stuart Schechter and John Outterbridge

51) The City of Pasadena Permit Center, on the left corner, was originally built to house the Gas Company and was designed in the Beaux-Arts style. The exterior decorative painting on the second story is called "graffito" and was created by an Italian immigrant. The Permit Center building was renovated in 1974. This building is listed on the National Register of Historic Places.

51) City of Pasadena Permit Center (originally the Gas Company Building), 1929, (architect unknown), 175 North Garfield Ave.

52) Pasadena Police Department Building, 1990, Stern-Ehrenkrantz/Kammages, a joint venture of Robert A.M. Stern Architects, New York and Ehrenkrantz/Kammages, Architects and Planners, San Francisco, 207 North Garfield Ave.

52) Next, on your left is the Pasadena Police Department Building, which is much newer than the others. Influenced by the older surrounding buildings and created to blend in with them, the design is a reinterpretation of those older styles from the 1920s. Known as Historic-Eclectic Postmodern, this type of architecture is inspired by historical architectural forms and reinterprets them for contemporary culture. Other examples of this style are the 1980s AT&T building in New York by the late Philip Johnson and the Disney Building in Burbank by Michael Graves.

In this structure, forms have been enlarged for effect. Notice the enormous scrolled volutes bracketing the walls, the large windows, and the big spheres. Housed within this building are the offices for the police as well as a small jail.

Pasadena Police Department Building

53) Pasadena Public Library, c. 1927, Myron Hunt and H.C. Chambers, 285 East Walnut Street

53) The Pasadena Public Library was designed combining elements of Italian and Spanish architecture. The arches in the center come from the Italian Renaissance and the sections on either side containing the large windows are similar to the Spanish Mission Revival style. This design was chosen from a competition. The previous building for the library, located at the corner of Walnut Street and Raymond Avenue, was designed circa 1887 in a Richardsonian Romanesque style by architect Henry Ridgeway. It suffered earthquake damage and was torn down. This building is listed as a Cultural Heritage Landmark by the City of Pasadena. This building is also listed on the National Register of Historic Places.

Pasadena Public Library

44

 Right on Walnut Street

 Right on Lake Avenue

**Left on California Blvd.
Left on Wilson Avenue**

54) On your right, at the corner of Los Robles Avenue, is the First Congregational Church. The church was designed in the English Gothic Revival style, which was very common for ecclesiastical buildings of the time. Some of the characteristics of the Gothic style of architecture are pointed arches and steeply pitched roofs. This is the "new" church built to replace an older structure, which was not located here. When this was built the population was growing and the church had to be enlarged. Architect Leon Caryl Brockway was a member of this church and he designed other structures in Pasadena as well.

55) Here on Lake Avenue, just past Del Mar Boulevard, is the Mid-century Modern Bullock's Pasadena (now Macy's), designed by Wurdeman and Becket. Elements of the Streamline Moderne style are blended here into a park-like setting and set above the ground level. Circular forms puncture the supports, lending a futuristic quality to the design. At the time of its completion, this store was considered to be the epitome of Modern design. This building is listed on the National Register of Historic Places.

56) On the corner is the California Institute of Technology. Cal Tech, as it is known, was founded by internationally accomplished astronomer George Ellery Hale. Hale was from Chicago and was educated at MIT. He thought that California should have a similar school. He was a trustee of the new school and chose the architects. Researchers from around the world have come to Cal Tech, including Albert Einstein and Linus Pauling, and many Nobel Prize winners and respected authors have been associated with the school. The student body consists of approximately 900 undergraduate students and 1200 graduate students, with a faculty of a little more than 900. Cal Tech is considered to be the premier school on the West Coast for the technical study of science, mathematics, and related fields.

George E. Hale originally chose Myron Hunt and Elmer Grey's firm, and the first building constructed, Gates Laboratory of Chemistry, was designed by them with Bertram G. Goodhue drawing the exterior details. Goodhue created a master plan for the campus and designed many of the buildings. The buildings were designed in a variety of styles, but the early concept put forth was to create a California style inspired by Spanish Renaissance architecture. Many influences are seen in the buildings here, such as Moorish, Pueblo, and European Beaux-Arts.

54) First Congregational Church, 1927, Leon Caryl Brockway and E.M. Patterson, 464 East Walnut Street

55) Bullock's Pasadena (now Macy's), 1947, Wurdeman and Becket, 401 South Lake Ave.

Some of the buildings seen from the street:

North Mudd, 1938, Goodhue Associates – The first building seen of a set, both with blue domes, second building in from the corner on your right, is known as North Mudd. Look around the window frames on the second floor here to see natural features such as waterfalls, canyons, and volcanoes depicted, alluding to the studies of historical geology. Various shell forms are also seen here. The faceted squares represent minerals and gems. On either side of the gems, in a vertical line, a chain of life is expressed, starting at the bottom with prehistoric beings, progressing to dinosaurs and mammoths, and ending with man on a horse.

West Kerckhoff (William G. Kerckhoff Laboratories of the Biological Sciences), 1928, Goodhue Associates – Next, another blue mosaic tiled domed portico punctuates the end of the structure. It is covered with extensive cast stone relief sculpture depicting the building's purpose as that of housing classrooms for the biological studies. Around the windows a vertical chain of monkeys, sea horses, crabs, lobsters, octopus, squid, and shell forms can be seen.

56a) California Institute of Technology – West Kerckhoff (William G. Kerckhoff Laboratories of the Biological Sciences), 1928, Goodhue Associates

56) California Institute of Technology, 1917-present, Various architects, bordered by California Blvd., Wilson Ave., Del Mar Blvd., and Hill Ave. – North Mudd, 1938, Goodhue Associates

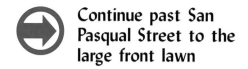 **Continue past San Pasqual Street to the large front lawn**

Beckman Institute, 1989, A.C. Martin & Associates – Next, set back from the street, the central scallop shell-form creates a focal point and the traditional open courtyard with arcades relates to the older buildings of the campus, defying the young age of this structure.

56b) California Institute of Technology – Beckman Institute, 1989, A.C. Martin & Associates

Broad Center for the Biological Sciences, 2002, Pei, Cobb, Freed – Here, adjacent to the previous structure is one of the more recently constructed buildings. Immediately apparent are the shiny etched stainless steel panels expressing the desire to portray a sense of cutting-edge scientific study, appropriate for the 21st century. However, travertine has also been used here to relate this building with the others.

Hale Solar Laboratory, 1924, Johnson, Kaufman & Coate – Located on the interior of the campus and not visible from the street, but necessary to mention. This laboratory has been designated a National Historic Landmark by the federal government. The laboratory is also listed on the National Register of Historic Places.

Athenaeum, 1930, Gordon Kaufman – This building is seen at the opposite end of the campus at the corner of Hill Avenue and California Boulevard. The Athenaeum is the most formal of all the structures and was designed in the European Beaux-Arts style, combining elements of Greek and Roman architecture with Andalusian and Mediterranean features. It is a meeting place for the faculty and contains housing, dining areas, and meeting rooms.

56d) California Institute of Technology – Athenaeum, 1930, Gordon Kaufman

56c) California Institute of Technology – Broad Center for the Biological Sciences, 2002, Pei, Cobb, Freed

Other architects who have designed buildings on the Cal Tech campus include Flewelling and Moody; Pereira and Luckman; Robert Alexander; Edward Durrell Stone; Moore, Ruble and Yudell; Hellmuth, Obata, and Kassabaum; and Neptune, Thomas, Davis. As the campus continues to evolve and expand, others will be added to this list.

 Right on Del Mar Blvd.

57) Here on your right, past Holliston Avenue, is a contemporary firehouse. Based on Cal Tech's master plan observing building heights, setbacks, and other requirements, the design concept was to create a unique building with its own individual character, yet blend with the eclectic nature of the existing buildings on the campus, as well as the residential buildings nearby. Of quasi-pyramidal form, with buttresses, flat roof, and asymmetrical massing, it has a strong street presence. The two-story scale is in keeping with the buildings of the neighborhood and the light beige color is close to that of many of the buildings on the Cal Tech campus. Depicting a sense of strength, yet not aggressive, it serves as home to the firefighters who work there.

58) The English Tudor Revival style house on your right is home to the Einstein Papers Project. This house was designed by the same architect who designed many homes in Pasadena, including the Wrigley Mansion, to be seen later. Originally a family home, it now serves as offices for an organization whose mission is to publish the entire archives of Albert Einstein. Einstein was in Pasadena from late 1930 to 1933. He came in the winters only and did not teach at the school, but was conducting research here and was most interested in the discoveries of the astronomers at Mt. Wilson, where the Hale telescope is located high in the mountains. The general editor of the archives publication is a professor at the school. The Einstein Papers Project was started in the late 1980s, but has been located here on the campus of Cal Tech since 2000.

Past San Pasqual Street, the Athenaeum (shown on opposite page) can be seen.

Athenaeum, 1930, Gordon Kaufman (part of the Cal Tech campus)

57) City of Pasadena Firehouse, 2002, Gonzalez/ Goodale, 1360 East Del Mar Blvd.

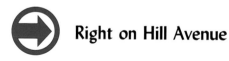

Right on Hill Avenue

58) Einstein Papers Project, c. 1917, G. Lawrence Stimson, 363 Hill Ave.

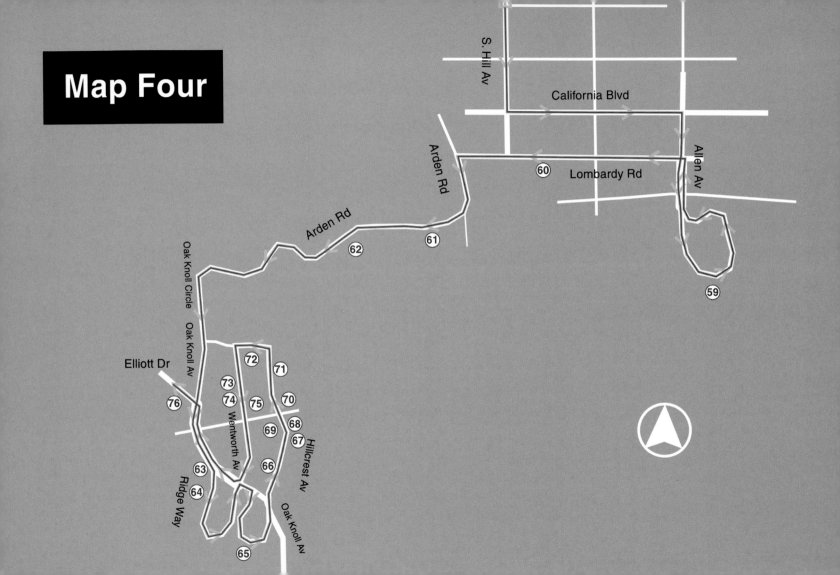

Map Four

S. Hill Av

California Blvd

Arden Rd

60 Lombardy Rd

Allen Av

Arden Rd

62

61

59

Oak Knoll Circle

Oak Knoll Av

Elliott Dr

72

71

73

74 75

70

76

69 68

67

Wentworth Av

Hillcrest Av

66

63

64

Ridge Way

Oak Knoll Av

65

Left on California Blvd. Right on Allen Ave. Through the iron gates to

59) The Huntington Library is located in the small city known as San Marino. San Marino was originally the name of the J. DeBarth Shorb Estate. Henry Huntington visited here and later purchased it in 1903. Incorporated in 1913, San Marino's population was listed as more than 13,000 in 2004. It covers 3.75 square miles.

The Huntington Library, Art Collections and Botanical Gardens were built in 1910 by architects Myron Hunt and Elmer Grey as a home for Henry Edwards Huntington, the wealthy railroad tycoon. Huntington owned the Pacific Electric Railway system after he inherited the Central Pacific Railroad from his uncle Collis P. Huntington. Henry Huntington had married his uncle's widow, Arabella Duval Huntington, and she was instrumental in developing their art collection. In 1920, Myron Hunt and H.C. Chambers designed the library. The home itself is now the art gallery. After Henry died in 1927, the estate was donated to the city and opened to the public. Most of the buildings have been designed in the European Beaux-Arts, or Neo-Classical style. The gardens and the grounds are extensive. The garden landscapes are derived from French, English, Japanese, Chinese, and Australian themes and also include Subtropical, Jungle, Herb gar-

dens and much more. There is a Japanese tea house, as well as the Huntington Mausoleum, designed in 1933 by John Russell Pope, who also designed the National Gallery in Washington D.C. The Gutenberg Bible can be seen in the exhibition rooms of the library, as well as Thoreau's *Walden*, Chaucer's *Canterbury Tales*, and Audubon's *Birds of America*, as well as many other rare books and manuscripts. Approximately 30,000 volumes on British and American art and literature are housed here. Highlights of the art collection include Thomas Gainsborough's *The Blue*

Boy and Sir Thomas Lawrence's *Pinkie*. There are also the works of other artists including Sir Joshua Reynolds, George Romney, John Constable and Joseph M.W. Turner. A collection of sculpture and decorative arts and a permanent exhibition of the work of architects Greene & Greene are housed here, too. Newer buildings on the grounds were designed by local architect Frederick Fisher and various others.

Huntington Library, Art Collections and Botanical Gardens

59) Huntington Library, Art Collections and Botanical Gardens, 1910, Myron Hunt and Elmer Grey, Library, 1920, Myron Hunt and H.C. Chambers, 1151 Oxford Road (entrance at Orlando Road and Allen Ave.)

**Circle around and exit onto Allen Avenue
Left on Lombardy Road
Pass Sierra Bonita Avenue**

On this street are elaborate homes designed by some of the most prominent architects of the time, including Reginald Johnson, Roland Coate, Myron Hunt, and Wallace Neff.

Continue on Lombardy Road

60) On your left is the Collins House designed in the Spanish Mediterranean Revival style. It is typical of the style that Neff preferred. He designed homes for the wealthy and famous including Mary Pickford, Douglas Fairbanks, and many others, but he also designed experimental housing, which you will see soon.

60) Wilbur W. Collins House, 1927, Wallace Neff, 1522 Lombardy Road

Left on Arden Road

61) Here on your left is an excellent example of a house designed in the Monterey Revival style. This style came from Monterey, California in the mid-19th century and resurfaced as a revival style in the 1920s. Complete with yellow glass lanterns and white gateposts, this style is characterized by the second story wraparound balcony and recessed lower level. This house resembles architectural styles in the South.

61) Paul J. Pitner House, 1928, Roland Coate, 1138 Arden Road

62) Next, on your left past Wilson Avenue, is a magnificent example of a half-timber English Tudor Revival style house. Half-timber was a method of construction which used both wood and masonry to create the striped pattern seen here. This house was originally a Craftsman style house designed by G. Lawrence Stimson in 1911, but was modified in the 1920s in this popular style.

62) Joseph Hixon House, c. 1925, Wendall W. Warren, 1050 Arden Road

First laid out by the Staats Realty Company, the Oak Knoll neighborhood you are entering now was originally a separate subdivision from Pasadena. The winding streets curve gracefully to accommodate the older trees and create a meandering movement. The homes and residents in this area were of the same caliber as those of Orange Grove Blvd., also known as Millionaire's Row. Prominent architects worked here, too, and a few examples of their work are highlighted.

 Left on Oak Knoll Circle (Becomes Oak Knoll Avenue) Right on Ridge Way

63) W. E. O'Brien House, 1912, Alfred and Arthur Heineman, 1327 South Oak Knoll Ave.

63) On the corner here on your right is the first example of the work of the Heineman Brothers, on this tour. The O'Brien House is unique with curved rooflines giving it the feel of a cottage. The multiple rooflines emphasize the parabolic curve at the peak; stylistically distinct from other Craftsman styles. More curvilinear than the houses of Greene & Greene, using varying rooflines, the composition of this house is more complex and dimensional. Not lived in for very long by the O'Briens, this house was sold in 1916 to Hugh McFarland for $27,500.

Brothers Alfred and Arthur Heineman were practicing at the same time as Greene & Greene and their firm was called A.S. Heineman & Company. They developed their own version of the Craftsman style. The brothers, who grew up in Pasadena, were not professionally trained as architects. Arthur did take the qualifying exam for registered architects and was granted that status even though he had no formal education. They were very prolific in Pasadena and Los Angeles and designed over 250 houses. You will see more of their work in this area.

64) Next door is another special house that was called "Idylwild." The most unique feature of this house is the use of logs both as horizontal and vertical elements, seen around the windows and doors. This is a more rustic version of Craftsman architecture.

The Milwaukee Building Company was one of the largest developers in Los Angeles in the early part of the 20th century. Architects and builders were employed to design and build numerous homes in a rapidly growing region. Eventually the name of the firm was changed to Meyer and Holler and they were responsible for the design of both the Egyptian and Chinese Theaters in Hollywood and many other structures throughout the area.

Around Ridge Way Right on Oak Knoll Avenue

65) Coming up quickly on the right is one of the grandest hotels in Pasadena. Originally called the Wentworth Hotel after its original owner, General Marshall Wentworth, it is now the Ritz-Carlton Huntington Hotel. Hotel developer Wentworth also built a number of hotels in the East and the Raymond Hotel here in Pasadena, which unfortunately burned to the ground. This hotel was sold to Henry Huntington circa 1913. Designed in 1906 in the Mission Revival style by Charles Whittlesey, who was from Chicago and worked in the office of the renowned architect Louis Sullivan. After Huntington bought it he had Myron Hunt redesign and expand the central section upwards. It opened again in 1914. The hotel was temporarily closed, dismantled and extensively rebuilt and restored in 1991 by McClellan, Cruz, Gaylord & Associates and DeBretteville, Polyzoides as historic consultants. It remains a magnificent and very sophisticated hotel. There is one particular feature contained on the grounds of the hotel that adds charm and character from an earlier era. The covered footbridge features murals created in the 1930s that depict various scenes of California by artist Frank Moore. Painted under the pitch of the roof, the murals are a nostalgic reminder of the early days of California.

64) Dr. F.K. Ledyard House, "Idylwild," 1909, W.F. Thompson for the Milwaukee Building Company, 1361 Ridge Way

65) Wentworth Hotel (now Ritz-Carlton Huntington Hotel), 1906, Charles F. Whittlesey; 1913, Myron Hunt; 1991, McClellan, Cruz, Gaylord & Associates; DeBretteville and Polyzoides, 1401 South Oak Knoll Ave.

Out of the hotel driveway Cross Oak Knoll Avenue Onto Hillcrest Avenue

66) This grand residence here on your left was commissioned by the prominent Landreth family. It was designed in the Colonial Revival style, seen more in the East Coast of this country, with Neo-Classical elements such as a triangular pediment and columns reminiscent of Greek architecture, but with an American flair. Harold Landreth, son of the original owner, went on to became a superior court judge.

66) Landreth House, c. 1918, Reginald D. Johnson, 1385 Hillcrest Ave.

67) Next on your right hidden behind the hedges and down the long driveway, is another by Greene and Greene, which was thought to be designed only by Henry Mather Greene. It was built for a judge in the Swiss Chalet-inspired Craftsman style.

67) William Ward Spinks House, 1909, Charles Sumner Greene & Henry Mather Greene, 1344 Hillcrest Ave.

68) Freeman House, 1913, Alfred and Arthur Heineman, 1330 Hillcrest Ave. This photo shows the house while it was undergoing restoration in 2006.

68) Another by the Heineman brothers is next on the right. The Freeman House, built in 1913, is another example of their Craftsman style. Originally built for James Allen Freeman, who was a retired lumber manufacturer from Arkansas, the house once sat on more than two acres and is over 11,000 square feet in size. Here, shingles are not used extensively; rather, half-timber construction is preferred, expressing the English influence. The parabolic peak on the roof is also evident in this house, as are the rolled eaves curving over the roof edges. On the interior, four Batchelder tile fireplaces helped to keep the house warm in winter. Some of the windows are from the locally renowned Judson Studios. The roof was meticulously restored in 2006 with cedar shingles, as was the half-timber exterior surface. This house has been declared a Cultural Heritage Landmark by the city of Pasadena.

69) Across the street on the corner is the Prindle House, thought to be designed by George Washington Smith of Santa Barbara in the Spanish Colonial Revival style. He was a master of this style and designed many buildings in Santa Barbara and Pasadena. This house was intended to be a replica of a particular house located in Spain.

69) William Prindle House, 1928, (attributed to) George Washington Smith, 1311 Hillcrest Ave.

 Continue on Hillcrest Avenue

70) Set back on your right is another house designed by Wallace Neff, here in the Italian Revival style. Unique to this house is its semi-circular shape, which surrounds a motor court, and if you look through the front door you can see through the back of the house. As Neff was known to do, this house was a replica of a Roman villa. The original owner was the granddaughter of brewer Adolphus Busch, who created Busch Gardens in the Lower Arroyo.

70) Mrs. Sydney Berg House, 1925, Wallace Neff, 1290 Hillcrest Ave

71) Next, coming up on your right is the Culbertson Sisters' House. (Another house of the Culbertson family, which was also designed by Greene & Greene, was seen earlier in the Park Place/Arroyo Terrace historic district.) Originally built for three sisters, Cordelia, Kate, and Margaret Culbertson, they sold the house in 1916 and moved to another Greene & Greene house in Pasadena. It is a very unique and unusual house in that it is covered in gunite and has a green glazed tile roof. It is not a typically recognizable Greene & Greene design. The Japanese influence is most evident here, more so than in any of the others designed by Greene & Greene. The house is U-shaped with an interior courtyard that can be seen through the front windows. Batchelder tiles were used on the interiors. It originally sat on several acres and there were once extensive gardens in the back, but the lot size is now approximately 30,000 square feet. This house is listed on the National Register of Historic Places.

71) Culbertson Sisters' House, 1911, Charles Sumner Greene & Henry Mather Greene, 1188 Hillcrest Ave.

72) Across the street, on the corner to your left, is what is considered to be the masterpiece of the work of Greene & Greene. Built for the owner of a lumber mill, who had originally hired architects Myron Hunt & Elmer Grey for the design of his house, the Blacker House is an elaborate culmination of the ideas of the Arts and Crafts home. Various influences are seen here, from Japanese and Swiss to Adirondack and Shingle styles. Originally, the main house, a garage, a groundskeeper's house, and a lath house (similar to a greenhouse), stood on more than five acres. A small lake and beautiful gardens once existed on the grounds, too. This was the largest wood house built by Greene & Greene and covers approximately 7,000 square feet. Around the corner we will see the former groundskeeper's quarters and garage. Once separately owned, the garage is now back as part of the original compound. On the inside, teak wall paneling was created and Douglas fir, mahogany, cedar, oak, and pine were used throughout. Integrated into the overall home design were furniture, decorative arts, lighting, art glass windows, murals, exposed joinery, and woodwork. After Mrs. Blacker died in the late 1940s, the land was divided into seven lots and the lath house was demolished. The other structures remain, but were sold off separately. The house was purchased in the 1980s by an insensitive owner who sold off the light fixtures, art glass, and other items from the house. The front door is a replica because he sold the original. The current owners purchased the house in 1994, painstakingly restoring it and incorporating the garage back into their property. This house is listed on the National Register of Historic Places.

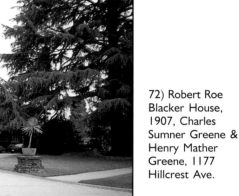

72) Robert Roe Blacker House, 1907, Charles Sumner Greene & Henry Mather Greene, 1177 Hillcrest Ave.

Robert Roe Blacker House

➡ Left on Wentworth Avenue

73) The house here on your right, down the driveway, was designed in the Mission Revival style reminiscent of the Spanish Missions, for A.K. Macomber, who only owned the house for a few years before selling it to Carl Lunkenheimer. Lunkenheimer was from Cincinnati, and his company was one of the largest brass manufacturers in the United States. He moved here and was planning on building a house of his own, but instead decided to buy this one. Architect Joseph J. Blick designed the Scottish Rite Cathedral, the Star-News Building, and hundreds of houses in Pasadena.

74) Next, on your right is another home by the Heineman brothers. Somewhat similar to the one we saw earlier, this home shows the influence of the English Arts & Crafts style. The architects perfected the rolled eaves of the parabolic curved overhanging roof, which serves to soften and refine the whole appearance of the house, while trying to imitate a thatched roof. Twelve layers of shingles were needed to create the rolled eaves here. "Eyebrows" are seen in the roof peeking out to the street, serving the function of air ventilation. On the inside, Batchelder tiles were used for decoration and leaded glass for the windows. Much of the Heineman Brothers' work is considered "transitional" because elements of the Victorian, English, and Craftsman styles are combined, which can be seen in this house. This house is listed on the National Register of Historic Places.

73) A.K. Macomber/Carl F. Lunkenheimer House, 1906, Joseph J. Blick, 1215 Wentworth Ave.

74) Edmunds House, c. 1917, Alfred and Arthur Heineman, 1233 Wentworth Ave.

75) Another Spanish Colonial Revival style house is on your left, designed by a firm of notable architects. Reginald Johnson's work has been seen earlier and will be seen again on this tour. Gordon Kaufman designed the Los Angeles Times building in Downtown L.A. and the Athenaeum at Cal Tech, and Roland Coate was known for his revival style homes here and in Los Angeles.

75) Joseph W. Campbell House, c. 1924, Johnson, Kaufman, Coate, 1244 Wentworth Ave.

**Right on Oak Knoll Avenue
Left on Elliott Drive
(sign for freeway)**

76) Here on your left is the Ross House, designed by Alfred and Arthur Heineman for a rancher named Winslow Ross at a cost of $8,000 in 1911. A combination of Asian, Neo-Classical, and Craftsman elements are used in this design. The elaborate open wood trusses in front have a distinctly Japanese origin; the Doric elephantine columns derive from Classical Greek and Roman architecture; while the dark wood shingles tie the house to its natural setting. The second floor bay window adds another dimension and may have been used as an open-air sleeping porch. The multiple rooflines also create a more visually complex composition. Inside, six different types of wood are used, and an inglenook around the fireplace decorated with Batchelder tiles is highlighted by a Plein Air mural. This house is listed on the National Register of Historic Places.

76) Ross House, 1911, Alfred and Arthur Heineman, 674 Elliott Drive

Map Five

Right on El Molino Avenue
Left on Glenarm Street
Left on Los Robles Avenue
Right on Wallis Street

77) Here on the right corner is another home designed by Wallace Neff. It has been called many things throughout the years, including The Bubble House and Dome House, and was built in 1946. Neff was trying new methods of building with low-cost concrete construction as a response to the housing shortage after World War II. Simply stated, this method of construction was carried out by inflating a balloon, applying a thin layer of concrete on top of it, deflating the balloon and then applying more concrete. On the inside, in just over 1,000 square feet, are two bedrooms and one bathroom, a kitchen, and a large living and dining room. Directly beneath the center of the dome is a fire pit with a tubular chimney creating a focal point inside. Some furniture was custom-made, like the bookshelves that curve around the outside walls. Also located on the property is a "bomb" or "fallout" shelter complete with a hatch in which one would enter the shelter, indicating the Post World War II attitude of the Cold War era.

Andrew Neff, the architect's brother, lived in this house and Wallace Neff moved into the house in 1975, where he spent much of the last years of his life. The house is a reflection of Neff's willingness to explore types of architecture that he was unaccustomed to using. Wallace Neff was much better known for his picturesque Spanish Colonial Revival and Mediterranean homes seen earlier. He thought everyone would want one of these houses, but unfortunately only one other in Pasadena was built, and it was later demolished. Some others were built outside the U.S., and a few more on the East Coast.

77) Airform House (a.k.a. Bubble House, Dome House), 1946, Wallace Neff, 1097 South Los Robles Ave.

Right on Marengo Avenue
Left on California Blvd.
Cross Orange Grove Blvd.
Left on Grand Ave.

78) The rustic cabin was the inspiration for this modest house on your left. Very much in keeping with the Craftsman sensibility of living with nature, Louis B. Easton built more than twenty other houses similar to this one, including his own house on South Marengo Avenue. He was sought after by middle class people to build modest homes. The wood was often left natural and the finish work left undone intentionally to achieve that rustic feeling. Easton came to Pasadena from the Chicago area as a child, and he was also a teacher and a furniture maker, but never a registered architect. The house has very deep, projecting eaves, allowing for the house to be shaded from the strong southern California sun and accommodating a front porch. Easton designed about twenty-five homes in Pasadena. Different from the architects who were designing for wealthy clients, he designed more modest and rustic homes for the working people. Thirteen of the homes he designed are still standing.

78)Volney H. Craig House, 1908, Louis B. Easton, 620 South Grand Ave.

In this neighborhood there are excellent examples of various Arts & Crafts style homes created from different influences and an elevated degree of preservation in these homes. Also found near the Arroyo are the archaeological discoveries of artifacts from the Native people who originally inhabited this area. This area is a historic district known as "Lower Arroyo Seco" and is listed on the National Register of Historic Places.

79) This house on your right was designed by architect Timothy Walsh for himself in his own version of the Craftsman style. The front entrance to this house is off to the side and away from the street. The composition of the front is asymmetrical. Very long barn shingles were used here on the second story and stucco on the first. Corner windows are also implemented here and somewhat unusual to see during this period. Walsh was originally from Boston, where he was well known.

79) Timothy Walsh House, c. 1907, Timothy Walsh, 619 South Grand Ave.

80) Right next door, the Austin House is remarkable for its unusual, flat, uncharacteristic roof. It has many elements of the Craftsman style and other styles too. With its board and batten vertical siding, latticework, and diamond pane windows, it is indeed a very unique house. The local story is that it was built as a gift for the daughter of Wilber Austin of Grable & Austin. She was a newlywed and the house was supposedly built while she was on her honeymoon. She wanted it to be unlike any other house and not require servants. It cost $2,000 to build.

Grable & Austin built more than thirty residences in Pasadena, both on speculation and for commissions. This house was built on a foundation of stones from the Arroyo Seco. The house right next door was also designed by Grable & Austin in the more traditional Craftsman style and was completely rebuilt after a fire.

 Right on La Loma Road

81) Another home by Timothy Walsh is here on your right, and again there are shingles on the second floor and the ground floor is surfaced in stucco, as seen before. Neo-Classical columns flank the entrance. This house was once owned by the prominent Van De Camp family who established a bakery in Los Angeles that operated for many years.

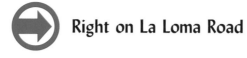

81) E.M. Wright House, c. 1907, Timothy Walsh, 691 La Loma Road

80) Austin House, 1907, Grable & Austin, 629 South Grand Ave.

 Continue on La Loma Road

As you cross the La Loma Bridge, look over the sides and you will see the more natural part of the Arroyo Seco. The Arroyo Seco is listed as a Cultural Heritage Landmark by the City of Pasadena. The bridge is listed on the National Register of Historic Places.

Cross bridge over Arroyo Seco Left on San Rafael Avenue

82) Your next site is down below on the right corner. This house was built in 1947 as one of the Case Study Houses. The Case Study House program was created by the editor of *Arts & Architecture* magazine as an attempt to create low-cost, post-war housing for southern California in response to the housing shortage after World War II. Known as Mid-Century Modern, this style attempts to pare down all decorative elements on the house and focus on the purity of the structure using straightforward forms and materials with no reference to a historic architectural style.

Continue on South San Rafael Avenue, just past Hillside Terrace

83) To your right on the corner is a magnificent study in horizontal sandstone, designed originally for Kenyon Reynolds and his wife. Reynolds was from Michigan and moved here with his family as a child. He was very successful in the gasoline business and also enjoyed tending extensive gardens on these grounds. After his wife died he became a priest, taught school in Canada, and wrote books. Architect Ogilvie was born in Scotland, but worked in the office of Reginald Johnson before opening his own practice. In this home he has captured the spirit of the British Manor house and countryside. The stone house, garage, and the landscaping create a romantic notion of home life and this house is like no other in the neighborhood. This architect designed many other houses mostly in Pasadena in various historical styles.

82) Case Study House #10, 1947, Kemper Nomland & Kemper Nomland, Jr., 711 South San Rafael Ave.

83) Kencott House (Kenyon L. Reynolds House), 1928, David Ogilvie, 901 South San Rafael Ave.

84) The Crowell House on your right reflects the Japanese-California ranch style house that was popular after World War II. Designed in the shape of an "L," the house extends in both directions and emphasizes the corner. Notice the double roof at the corner. Exposed rafter tails and simplicity of form express a casual outdoor California lifestyle.

Whitney R. Smith was a native of Pasadena and an instructor at the prestigious University of Southern California (USC). His architecture firm designed many homes in the Mutual Housing Association in the Brentwood Hills of Los Angeles, which was an ambitious housing project in the 1950s, and the Neighborhood Church seen earlier on the tour. They also designed 250 individual houses in the U.S. and won an award from the National AIA in cooperation with *House and Home* and *Sunset* magazines in 1956.

84) Crowell House, 1952, Smith and Williams (Whitney R. Smith), 949 South San Rafael Ave.

Continue as the street curves

85) Finally, at the end of the street on your right is the Gallion House. It was designed by a city planner who was also the dean of the School of Architecture at USC from 1945-1960. Before that he was the Director of Development for the Federal Public Housing Authority from 1936-1945. His own house here demonstrates a distinctly Asian style. The roof, with its concrete crown molding, is covered in fish scale terra cotta tiles, with flame-like flares at the tips. The square windows are covered with a fanciful concrete swirling openwork design to let in light, and the garage doors are wood paneled. This decoration owes its influence to those styles found in Thailand and is very unique to the neighborhood.

85) Gallion House, 1956, Arthur B. Gallion, 1055 South San Rafael Ave.

**Left on Laguna Road
Cross over bridge
Left on Arroyo Blvd.
Continue to bear left
on Arroyo Blvd.
Pass Busch Place
Just past Garden Lane**

86) The house with the semi-circular frosted glass windows on your left is part of the remains of the Grecian pergola that served as the entrance to Busch Gardens. Financed by Adolphus Busch, the beer brewer from St. Louis, thirty acres of beautifully landscaped gardens, fountains, paths, ponds, grazing sheep, fairy tale figures, and miniature houses extended from his own home high above on Orange Grove Blvd. into the Arroyo. Busch Gardens opened in 1906 and was a tourist attraction for many years until it closed in the late 1930s and the land was subdivided.

87) The house here on your right is the Lansing and Katharine Beach residence, designed in the French Norman Revival style. The Lansings met in Europe during WWI. She was an ambulance driver and he was a Lieutenant Colonel. He was from New York and she was from Indiana, and when they returned from the war they were married. The Beach's commissioned the firm of Witmer & Watson to design a home that reminded them of where they met. David Witmer also designed the Pentagon in Washington D.C.

86) Busch Gardens Grecian Pergola, c. 1906, Frederick L. Roehrig, 1025 South Arroyo Blvd.

87) Beach House, 1927, David Witmer and Loyall Watson, 760 South Arroyo Blvd.

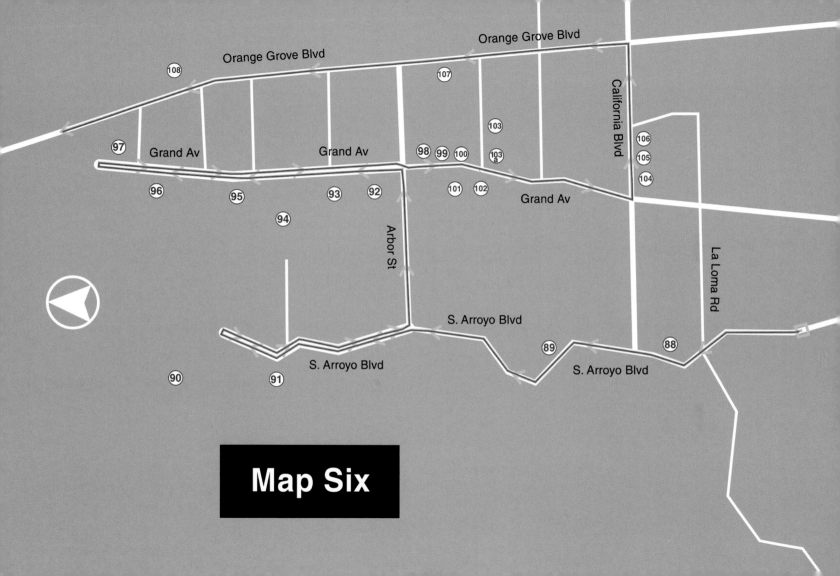

Orange Grove Blvd

Orange Grove Blvd

108

107

California Blvd

97 Grand Av   Grand Av   98 99 100   106

103   105

103
a   104

96   101 102   Grand Av

95   93   92

94

Arbor St

S. Arroyo Blvd

La Loma Rd

89   88

S. Arroyo Blvd

90   91   S. Arroyo Blvd   S. Arroyo Blvd

Map Six

 **Pass La Loma Road**

88) Next, here on your right is the home of Ernest Batchelder. He was a very successful decorative tile maker and had one of the major tile manufacturing firms in the area. It was considered then, and is now, prestigious to have Batchelder tiles in your home. He created the tiles here and the original kiln used to be in the backyard. Tile fountains, wishing wells, and paths all make use of this decorative medium here. The house itself is clad in narrow brown shingles and gunite. In 1916 the second story was added. Other alterations have been made, too. Unfortunately, the effects of the Great Depression destroyed his business. However, Batchelder was also an author of books on design and was the head of the design department of Throop Polytechnic Institute. At this location he started a school and studio. His wife Alice Coleman founded the Coleman Chamber Music Series. This house is listed as a Cultural Heritage Landmark by the City of Pasadena. It is also listed on the National Register of Historic Places.

88) Ernest A. Batchelder House, 1909, Ernest A. Batchelder – Builder, 626 South Arroyo Blvd.

Ernest A. Batchelder House

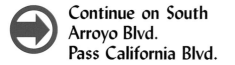

Continue on South Arroyo Blvd. Pass California Blvd.

89) The house here on your right was designed for artist Jean Mannheim. Mannheim was a respected member of the California Plein Air Painters and his

paintings now sell for tens of thousands of dollars. Originally from Germany, he came to Pasadena in 1908 and lived here for over 30 years. His paintings reflect the natural landscape of the Arroyo that inspired him. Inside, there is an open studio in the living room with large skylights to allow the natural light in. The current owner purchased the home from the daughters of Mannheim in 1987. This house is listed as a Cultural Heritage Landmark by the City of Pasadena.

89) Jean Mannheim House and Studio, 1909, Jean Mannheim, (attributed to) Louis du Puget Millar, John S. Walter – Builder, 500 South Arroyo Blvd.

The Lower Arroyo was an artist's colony and many painters and artisans lived in this area in the early part of the 20th century. This was a neighborhood of Bohemians attracted by the natural beauty of the Arroyo Seco. The California Plein Air Painters were artists who painted landscapes and seascapes and were active from the late 1890s into the 1920s. This version of American Impressionism focused on the natural beauty of the untouched environment. Residents besides Jean Mannheim who lived here include artists Guy Rose, husband and wife Marion and Elmer Wachtel, and sculptor Alexander Stirling Calder, father of the well-known mobile artist. Helen Lukins Gaut lived here, too. She was a writer of articles about homes and gardens for magazines such as Pasadena Beautiful and Cosmopolitan.

Continue on South Arroyo Blvd.

90) The Colorado Street Bridge was needed to connect Pasadena to Los Angeles and span the Arroyo Seco. It was constructed of reinforced concrete and is 28 feet wide, 1476.5 feet long, has 48 lamps and 11 parabolic arches. The elegant design of the bridge sets it apart from others and at the time of its construction, it was the tallest concrete bridge. In the late 1930s, steel fencing was added to the original concrete balustrade railing. The residents of Pasadena, along with governmental organizations, are very protective of their beloved bridge. It was through their efforts that it was fully restored and seismically upgraded in 1993. A celebration is held on the bridge every summer, hosted by Pasadena Heritage, highlighting its design and history. The California Department of Transportation has deemed this bridge one of the state's historically significant bridges. One of the reasons for this was that in 1915, just after the bridge was completed, there were more car owners in Pasadena than anywhere else in the world! This structure is listed as a Cultural Heritage Landmark by the City of Pasadena. This structure is also listed on the National Register of Historic Places.

90) Colorado Street Bridge, 1913, Waddell & Harrington (John Alexander Lowe Waddell, engineer), John Drake Mercereau Bridge and Construction Company, designer

91) Across from Westbridge Place, here on your left through the gated driveway is La Casita Del Arroyo, built to be used as a public meeting place. This house was built through a joint project of the Pasadena Garden Club and the government during the Great Depression to create jobs for unemployed people. This is a very different type of structure designed by Myron Hunt, who donated his services for this project and whose work you have seen earlier. The stones used in the construction of the house are from the Arroyo down below, as well as trees that were found on the ground and sand. Some of the wood was salvaged from various sites. An early recycling project, the house has been used as a meeting place for the Pasadena Garden Club. This building is listed as a Cultural Heritage Landmark by the City of Pasadena.

91) La Casita del Arroyo, c. 1934, Myron Hunt, 177 South Arroyo Blvd.

**U-turn in driveway
Right on South Arroyo
Blvd.
Left on Arbor Street
Left on Grand Avenue**

92) Here on your left is the Staats House. William Staats was born in Connecticut and came to Pasadena for his health and to start a business in 1887. He established the well-known William R. Staats Company, a real estate concern. He was chosen by Henry Huntington to subdivide and sell the Oak Knoll area. This house was designed in the French Provincial Revival style popular in the 1920s.

92) William R. Staats House, 1924, Marston, Van Pelt, and Maybury, 293 South Grand Ave.

93) Next, on your left is the pink-hued Tod Ford, Jr. House, designed in the Spanish Mediterranean Revival style. On this site was once a house designed by Greene & Greene, which was torn down by Tod Ford, Jr. so this one could be built. Ford held many prestigious titles including assistant director of the National Research Council in Washington D.C. He was also president of the Fencing Club, a member of the Midwick Country Club, and an aviator in France.

94) On your left, far back at the edge of the Arroyo behind the hedges, is a house that was designed using the half-timber method for the son of a railroader. Born in Ohio, Henry Robinson came to Pasadena to retire. He was a lawyer, in earlier days, and helped in the formation of the U.S. Steel company. While here he was a trustee of Cal Tech and a friend of Henry Huntington.

95) Next door is the Shakespeare Club, which was designed in the Italian Renaissance Revival style. It stands out as very unique amongst the other architectural types on this street. This building was originally the home of Mrs. Henry Everett, who came here to spend the winters away from her home in New York. She hosted many social gatherings and musical events here. At one time the Jet Propulsion Lab was housed here, but in 1972 the Shakespeare Club moved in. The club began in the late 1880s and is one of the oldest women's organizations. The purpose of the club is to uphold the "cultural, educational and philanthropic interests of its members."

93) Tod Ford, Jr. House, c. 1917, Reginald D. Johnson, 257 South Grand Ave.

94) Henry Robinson House, c. 1905, Charles Sumner Greene & Henry Mather Greene, 195 South Grand Ave.

95) Shakespeare Club, c. 1925, Marston, Van Pelt & Maybury, 171 South Grand Ave.

96) Again on your left, the Vista del Arroyo Hotel (now the U.S. Court of Appeals) was designed in 1915-1920 by various local architects in the Spanish Colonial Revival style. This hotel had its beginnings as a boarding house and then grew into a grand hotel built during the era of tourism in Pasadena. There were also bungalows and gardens on the grounds. The hotel prospered and a tower was built in 1930 to take advantage of the views. It was considered to be one of Pasadena's most fashionable hotels, but in 1943 the United States Army took over and used it as a military hospital called the McCornack Army Hospital. In 1985 it was renovated and is now used as the United States Court of Appeals. This building is listed on the National Register of Historic Places.

96)The Vista del Arroyo Hotel, (now United States Court of Appeals), c. 1915; Expansion 1920, Marston, Van Pelt & Maybury, Myron Hunt and Hunt & Chambers, 125 South Grand Ave.

97) On your right, past Green Street, is a condominium complex designed to blend in with the neighborhood. It is tucked into the landscaping and the units are graduated back on the property.

97) Vista Grande Condominiums, c. 1981, Buff and Hensman, 78-108 South Grand Ave.

 Turn around at the end of the street Continue back down Grand Avenue

98) On your left, just past Arbor Street, the Seifert House is unique with its flat roof, although it does blend in with the Craftsman style of the neighborhood. This is a very good example of how a modern house built much later than most of the others in the area can be made to blend in yet have its own identity. There are many Craftsman elements, yet it is a distinctly modern house. This property was once part of the lot next door.

98) R.J. Seifert House, c. 1964, John C. Egan, 356 South Grand Ave.

99) Next on your left is the George B. Post House, designed in the Shingle Style. This house changed hands frequently in its early days and was once owned by Tracy Drake, who was the president of the Drake Hotel in Chicago and spent the winters here, but it was originally built for George Post. The Shingle Style is similar to the Craftsman style, but shows more of the influence of Victorian architecture. This style was more fashionable at the turn of the century in the East and Midwest than it ever was here. The work of this architect was seen earlier in the Oak Knoll area.

99) George B. Post House, 1903, Joseph J. Blick, 360 South Grand Ave.

100) Next on the left is a house designed by G. Lawrence Stimson, the same builder who built the Wrigley Mansion, which you will soon see. The Stimson Company built many houses on speculation, as was this one. The house had a number of different owners and Stimson did not live here.

100) G. Lawrence Stimson Company House, 1910, G. Lawrence Stimson – Builder, 390 South Grand Ave.

101) Frank C. Bolt House, "Cobbleoak," 1893, Jasper Newton Preston and Seymour Locke, 395 South Grand Ave.

101) Across the street is the Bolt House, also known as "Cobbleoak," one of the oldest houses on this street and designed in 1893 by Seymour Locke and Jasper Newton Preston in the Late Victorian era. It is a wonderful combination of stone and wood construction, presumably with stones from the Arroyo. Frank C. Bolt was a banker and businessman and was president of the San Gabriel Bank. Originally from New York, as a young boy he carried mail for the army during the Civil War and witnessed Abraham Lincoln's final speech. The home's original design has been altered by subsequent owners, but what remains is a very unique house. The family of one of the architects, Seymour Locke, owned sixteen acres nearby and Locke Haven Street in this neighborhood was named after them.

102) Next door, the Francis House was built for the son of the former governor of Missouri, in the American Colonial or Georgian Revival style. Originally on this site was the house of the architect's father, Bishop Johnson, but it was demolished so this one could be built.

103) The house around the corner was moved to this location in 1982 from the area outside of Downtown L.A. Beautifully restored, it was designed in the Late Victorian style with the typical tall and narrow form, 2 1/2 stories with balconies, and an oriel window on the second floor. A bay window and elaborate decoration distinguish the front entrance, and the entire house is covered in clapboard siding and shingles.

103a) Next is another house also moved to this location. This one was designed in a transitional style, combining elements of English Tudor Revival with half-timber yellow and gold decoration under the roof pitch, front facing gable, a Craftsman type stone chimney, shingles, Neo-Classical dentil molding (looking like teeth), painted panels, and columns at the front entrance. This style was seen between and overlapping the periods of Victorian and Craftsman architecture, adding even more variety to this richly diverse neighborhood.

102) Sidney R. Francis House, 1929, Reginald D. Johnson, 415 South Grand Ave.

103) Victorian House, c. 1887, Merithew and Ferris, 510 Locke Haven

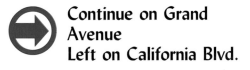

103a) Transitional Style House, c. 1903, W.B. Edwards, 440 South Grand Ave.

➡ **Continue on Grand Avenue**
Left on California Blvd.

108) The Ambassador Foundation purchased these grounds in the 1940s and tried to incorporate the new buildings of their campus with some of the original houses already existing here. They also built Ambassador College and The Ambassador Auditorium, which was closed in 1990. The Harvest Rock Church now owns the Ambassador Auditorium, located within the grounds here. The landscaping plan was originally designed by well-known Modern landscape architect Garrett Eckbo. Some of the structures on the campus grounds are:

108) Ambassador Foundation/Worldwide Church of God; Ambassador College Campus, Various dates, Various architects, corners of Orange Grove Blvd., Green Street and St. John Ave.

Fine Arts and Sciences Building (white honeycomb), c. 1967, Daniel, Mann, Johnson and Mendenhall
The Ambassador Auditorium, 1974, Daniel, Mann, Johnson and Mendenhall
Scofield House, 1909, Frederick L. Roehrig
Sprague House, 1903, A.A. Sprague
Merritt House, c. 1906, W.F. Thompson

108a) Ambassador Campus – Fine Arts and Sciences Building (white honeycomb), c. 1967, Daniel, Mann, Johnson and Mendenhall

108b) Ambassador Campus – Merritt House, c. 1906, W.F. Thompson

Easily seen from the street on Orange Grove Blvd. is the Fine Arts and Sciences Building (white honeycomb) and the Merritt House. (To see the other structures you must walk into the campus.) The Fine Arts and Sciences Building has a futuristic look with a cellular, or honeycomb, module repeated. Located in the middle of these two newer buildings is the Merrit House. Dating from more than fifty years earlier, it has a large, curved front portico and a Neo-Classical inspired design. This house once stood alone and was part of the collection of mansions on "Millionaire's Row."

The future of the built environment in Pasadena will continue to evolve. New projects in the planning stages include five buildings at Cal Tech, one of which will be designed by New York-based architect Joshua Prince-Ramus, a partner of Dutch architect Rem Koolhaas. Another architect working on a building at CalTech is Thom Mayne of Morphosis, based in Los Angeles, who was recently awarded the highest honor in architecture – the Pritzker Prize – and who in 2004 completed the CalTrans District Headquarters in Downtown L.A., one of the city's most innovative buildings. Architect Frank Gehry, designer of Walt Disney Concert Hall, also in Downtown L.A., will be designing a building at the Art Center College of Design campus here as well. Pasadena's strong sense of historic preservation has made the city a three-dimensional history of architecture for the past one hundred years. With contemporary buildings currently being added to the structural landscape, hopefully the city will become a visual history of the next one hundred years and beyond.

Selected Bibliography

Bosley, Edward, R. *Greene & Greene*. London: Phaidon Press Limited, 2000.

City of Pasadena Architectural and Historical Inventory Survey Area Twenty-One Bungalow Heaven Neighborhood Volume I, Urban Conservation Program, City of Pasadena, April 1987.

City of Pasadena Architectural and Historical Inventory Survey Area Twenty-One Bungalow Heaven Neighborhood Volume II, Urban Conservation Program, City of Pasadena, April 1987.

Gebhard, David, and Robert Winter. *Los Angeles An Architectural Guide*. Layton, Utah: Gibbs Smith Publisher, 1994.

Lowery, Lucie Marsh. Pasadena-Heritage to High Tech; "Partners In Excellence" by Robert J. Kelly and Sharon Makokian. Canoga Park, California: CCA Publications, 1993.

Magilligan, Robert J. *A Garden Of Homes: Charles and Henry Greene Create an Earthly Paradise*. Pasadena, California: Self-Published, 2004.

Makinson, Randell L., Thomas A. Heinz, Brad Pitt. *Greene & Greene: The Blacker House*. Layton, Utah: Gibbs Smith Publisher, 2000.

Myers, Kirk. *When Old Town was Young: The Early Decades of Old Pasadena*. Pasadena: Kirk Myers, 1994.

Pasadena Heritage Archives

Pasadena Museum of History Archives

Ripley, John. *Grable & Austin, Pasadena Builders*. Pasadena, 1994-2004.

Robinson, W.W. *Pasadena: A Calendar of Events in the Making of a City*. Los Angeles: Title Insurance and Trust Company, 1955.

Sheid, Ann. *Pasadena: Crown of the Valley An Illustrated History*. Northridge, California: Windsor Publications, 1986.

Sillo, Terry & John Manion. *Around Pasadena – An Architectural Study*. Pasadena: Gallery Productions, 1976.

Wayte, Beverly. *At the Arroyo's Edge: A History of Linda Vista*. Los Angeles, California: Historical Society of California and Linda Vista/Annandale Association, 1992.

Index